D0753624

The Library of HOLIDAYS™

Earth Day

Amy Margaret

The Rosen Publishing Group's
PowerKids Press
New York

For Chloe Nicole

Published in 2002 by The Rosen Publishing Group, Inc.
29 East 21st Street, New York, NY 10010

First Edition

Book Design: Michael Caroleo and Michael de Guzman
Project Editors: Jennifer Landau, Jason Moring, Jennifer Quasha

Photo Credits: pp. 4, 19 © AFP/CORBIS; p. 7 © SuperStock; p. 8 © AP Photo/Steve Tomasko; p. 11 © Bettmann/CORBIS; p.12 © Frank Leonardo/Archive Photos; p. 15 © Todd Gipstein/ CORBIS; p. 16 © Skjold Photography; p. 20 © D. Robert Franz/CORBIS; p. 22 © Joseph Sohm; ChromoSohm Inc./CORBIS.

Margaret, Amy.
Earth day / by Amy Margaret.— 1st ed.
     p. cm. — (The library of holidays)
Includes bibliographical references and index.
  ISBN 0-8239-5787-X (lib. bdg. : alk. paper)
1. Earth Day—Juvenile literature. 2. Environmentalism—United States—Juvenile literature.
3. Environmental protection—United States—Juvenile literature. [1. Earth Day. 2. Environmental protection. 3. Holidays.] I. Title.
  GE195.5 .M36 2002
  333.7—dc21
                                                                               00–013022

Manufactured in the United States of America

Contents

All About Earth Day

The first Earth Day was held in 1970 to draw attention to the need to care for our planet. **Littering** and **pollution** were becoming a problem in the United States and other places around the world. People were being wasteful with materials. Very few people **recycled**. Earth Day changed all that. As of 1990, the holiday of Earth Day is held on April 22 of each year all over the world.

◀ *There are many fun ways to celebrate Earth Day. In this picture, kids are playing with a model of planet Earth.*

How Earth Has Changed

Over time, the number of people that live on Earth has grown to more than 5 billion. This has made the Earth's land, air, and water change. The air has become **polluted** with the exhaust from millions of cars, trains, and buses. Rivers, lakes, and oceans have become **contaminated** with chemicals and waste. With so many people using so many materials, the number of garbage dumps and **landfills** has become huge.

From top to bottom, these are pictures of a garbage dump, waste spilling into a water source, and traffic causing air pollution. ▶

Gaylord Nelson, Earth Day Founder

A man named Gaylord Nelson first thought of Earth Day. Gaylord became a U.S. senator for Wisconsin in 1962. He thought that protecting the **environment** was an important issue. He spoke to the Senate about the environment. Not many politicians seemed interested in hearing what Gaylord had to say. This didn't stop Gaylord from fighting to protect the country's land, water, and wildlife.

◀ *This is a picture of Gaylord Nelson, who came up with the idea for Earth Day.*

9

As a U.S. senator, Gaylord Nelson, the **founder** of Earth Day, tried to get help for the environment from people throughout the country. In 1969, Gaylord heard about a big oil leak off the coast of southern California. The leak hurt the oceans. Gaylord was so upset that he put together a nationwide **demonstration** about the environment. He announced that it would be held in spring 1970. This was the birth of Earth Day.

10

Top: *The duck shown was covered in oil after a spill in California in 1969.* Bottom: *These men are raking oil-soaked hay after an oil spill near a shoreline.* ▶

Earth Day, 1970

The first Earth Day was April 22, 1970. More than 20 million people throughout the United States took part. In New York City, people weren't allowed to drive cars along a major road called Fifth Avenue. This showed people how quiet the streets could be without cars driving down them. Because of Earth Day, the Environmental Protection Agency (EPA), a new government agency, was started. The EPA tries to stop cities and companies from polluting.

◀ *This is a picture of people walking down Fifth Avenue in New York City on the first Earth Day in 1970. Cars were not allowed to drive down the avenue on Earth Day.*

Earth Day, 1990

The second Earth Day was celebrated on April 22, 1990. Its saying was "Think **Globally** . . . Act Locally." This means that to fix the world each person must do his or her part. This time 200 million people all around the world were involved in Earth Day.

Gaylord Nelson was the honorary **chairman** of this second Earth Day. He spoke to groups about working to save the Earth. Since Earth Day, 1990, Earth Day has been held every year on April 22.

The people shown here are standing outside the Capitol in Washington, D.C. They are celebrating Earth Day, 1990. ▶

What You Can Do for Earth Day

Make Earth Day an important day each year. Choose an environmental issue that you care about, such as air pollution, protection of wildlife, or saving trees. With friends, think about ways you can help your cause. For example, you can write letters to local businesses and ask them to **donate** a tree. Then on Earth Day, you and your friends can plant the trees. To cut down on air pollution, you can put together a carpool day in honor of Earth Day.

◄ *One Earth Day activity is to help clean up your local park.*

Earth Day Around the World

Today Earth Day takes place in almost every country in the world. Everyone honors this day in different ways. In Korea, 16 cities hold a car-free day for Earth Day. No cars can be driven for the whole day. In 2000, the United Kingdom held an Eco-**festival**. More than 40,000 people attended. In Peru, 5,000 children planted 1,000 trees around the city. Each year the celebration of Earth Day grows.

In this picture, Chinese families gather to bury a rock in honor of Earth Day. At this event, trees were planted on top of the spot where the rock was buried. ▶

Make Every Day Earth Day

Earth Day may be celebrated on only one day of the year, but you can honor Earth Day every day. You can reuse grocery bags from the store. Don't forget to recycle cans and newspapers, too. To cut down on litter in your neighborhood, just pick it up! You can save water by taking shorter showers. Don't leave the water running while you brush your teeth. Look around your own neighborhood and see what you can do to make your part of the world a better place to live.

◀ *The boys shown here are collecting litter from the roadside during Earth Day, 1990.*

Groups That Protect Our Earth

Many groups work to keep Earth a safe, healthy place to live. The National Wildlife Federation works to protect our environment. They have fought to save many places and types of wildlife threatened by businesses. Their Web site is www.nwf.org. The Sierra Club teaches people how to use Earth's **resources** carefully. Their Web site is www.sierraclub.org. Contact these groups and others to find out how you can help them do their important work.

Glossary

chairman (CHAYR-man) A person in charge of a meeting or an event.

contaminated (kun-TA-mih-nayt-ed) When something is made unusable by the adding of poisonous or undesirable elements.

donate (DOH-nayt) To give something away.

demonstration (deh-mun-STRAY-shun) A way of showing people how to do something by acting it out.

environment (en-VY-urn-ment) All the living things and conditions that make up a place.

festival (FES-tih-vul) A day or special time of rejoicing or feasting.

founder (FOWN-der) The person who starts or establishes an event.

globally (GLO-bah-lee) Having to do with the whole world.

landfills (LAND-filz) Layers of Earth in which waste is buried.

littering (LIH-ter-ing) Throwing unneeded materials in places where they don't belong.

polluted (puh-LOOT-ed) Made unclean by human-made waste.

pollution (puh-LOO-shin) Human-made waste that hurts the environment.

recycled (ree-SY-kuhld) Reused.

resources (REE-sors-es) Supplies of energy and useful materials.

23

Index

A
air pollution, 6, 17

C
chemicals, 6

E
Eco-festival, 18
environment, 9, 10, 22
Environmental Protection Agency (EPA), 13

L
landfills, 6, 9
litter(ing), 5, 21

N
National Wildlife Federation, The, 22
Nelson, Gaylord, 9, 10, 14
New York City, 13

P
pollution, 5, 6, 13, 17

R
recycling, 5, 21

S
Sierra Club, The, 22

T
trees, saving, 17

W
waste, 6
water, 6, 9, 21
wildlife, 9, 17, 22

Web Sites

Due to the changing nature of Internet links, PowerKids Press has developed an online list of Web sites related to the subject of this book. This site is updated regularly. Please use this link to access the list: www.powerkidslinks.com/lhol/earth/

24